IT WAS ME

Carolyn V. Williams

WRITING In FAITH

©2016 by Carolyn V. Williams
All rights reserved, including the right to reproduce this book or portions thereof in any form whatsoever by author. No part of this book may be reproduced, scanned, or distributed in any print or electronic form without permission. Please do not participate, or encourage piracy of copyrighted materials in violation of author's rights.

Scripture quotations are taken from The Holy Bible, King James Version

Library of Congress Cataloging-in Publication Data
ISBN 978-0-9974047-0-8

Carolyn V. Williams (text, poem)
IT WAS ME

Dedication

This book is dedicated in the memory of Chad V. Williams Sr.-aka "STUNNA", my one and only son. I will love you always and forever. I want to also acknowledge my daughter Andrea, whom I know misses her brother more than she says. Andrea, you have stood by my side to wipe every tear I have shed and you are my reason now for living (I love you baby girl). To Peggy my mother, R.I.P .You will always be the wind beneath my wings, and my highest guardian angel in heaven. Your spirit continues to guide me through your soft whispers of love, and I can feel your presence daily. To my mentors, Arthur "Silky Slim" Reed, you pulled the vision out of me by encouraging me to face my inner fears. To Rev. King and my Sissy, who earnestly encouraged me to never give up on my dreams.I can't forget about my faithful and dedicated members of Healing Hearts. I could never thank you guys enough for believing in me, thank you for walking this journey with me, for we all have been there. To my loving family, my grandchildren (Chad Jr., Cha'Kari, Chadrenea, Chadler) and my new found family & friends, from day one you guys never complained when I would have those days of uncontrollable grief. You lent me your shoulders to cry on and you always listened as I talked and mourned about my Chad. You guys were and are still my rock, and it's because of all of you that I choose to LIVE, LOVE and REJOICE!

<u>Deuteronomy 1:6 (KJV)</u>

The Lord our God said to us at Horeb, "You have stayed long enough at this mountain".

Contents

Dedication……………………………………………..
It Was Me…………………………………………...……1

Unconditional Love…………………………………….17
Acceptance……………………………. ……………...18
The Formation of Healing Hearts…………………19
Testimonies……………………………………………21
Accepting God's Will……………………………………24
Special Dedication to Mothers…………. …………….25
Resources   ………………………………………….26

A mother named Carol-lou sits on the edge of her bed night after night watching the local news about the violence happening in her home town. In thinking to herself, she would say, "Lord, some mothers heart is hurting tonight." Just before drifting off into a deep sleep, she would always whisper a silent prayer. Praying for the mother in each story with a different face whom she had seen time after time again on the news and her son, wondering how that mother felt knowing that her son wouldn't make it home that night.

Carol-lou had a son named Verdell. Verdell was tall for his age. He was 6"2 to be exact. He was handsome with a sweet spirit that charmed everyone he met. Verdell was always polite and he had good manners. He knew that Carol-lou and his grandmother (Mama) didn't play. They had both taught him very well and he loved both of them dearly.

However, everyone knew Mama was his favorite girl and that Mama's eyes were not big enough to see Verdell, because he was the apple of her eye.

Carol-lou and Mama watched Verdell sprout into a fine teenager. Knowing the dangers he would have to face as a young black man growing up in this world, they would often talk with him about the violence in the streets. Their hopes were that he would have a bright future in this world. Verdell's outgoing personality led them both to think that whatever he did, whether it was football, work or school, that he would be successful and one day take care of them. Carol-lou prayed that he had listened to what she and Mama had talked with him about earlier that day. As usual, she whispered a silent prayer that night and drifted off to sleep. Verdell was growing older now, and the thought scared

Carol-lou as he grew. Carol-lou asked him about some of the things he saw and heard in the streets. She listened attentively as her son talked about how his friends indulged in drugs and alcohol. She gazed at him with a concerned smile and folded arms, rocking nervously as she continued to listen. She didn't want to fuss with Verdell, and she was pleased that her son trusted her enough to share the things he was experiencing in the streets, but it also filled her with great fear. One day, after one of their mother and son talks, he picked her up and hugged her tight like a bear. He looked her in her eyes and said, "Man Moms stop tripping, I'm a good boy, I'm not in those streets." Kissing her gently on the cheek he whispered "I love you Mom." When Verdell turned 18, so did his attitude. He became disobedient; he began talking back and not wanting to listen to Mama or Carol-lou about his friends or his girl-friends. In the mist of this change Mama died. Shortly after that Verdell's first child was born.

Needless to say, Verdell wasn't dealing with the loss of his Mama well. He began getting in trouble, hanging out on the corners, as well as consuming alcohol and drugs with his friends. Late in the mid-night hours Carol-lou could expect her phone to ring. It would be Verdell on the line, crying about how he didn't want to live without his Mama. Often he would say, "I would give anything but my kid to be with Mama." Carol-lou knew in her heart that Verdell was depressed and missing his Mama. Patiently she would listen and tell him, "Verdell, Mama would want you to live, not be with her." Nothing seemed to ease his pain.

"Mama"

Carol-lou grew more fragile and weaker, for she too was missing her mom just as much. Doing what any other mother would do, she cried and prayed. Trying to ease Verdell's pain through his difficult time, she bought him cars, rims, music and whatever else she felt would ease

Verdell's pain. It eventually became clear to her a few months later that nothing she did would be able to ease his pain or bring his Mama back. Carol-lou grew very scared. She knew more so now than ever that her preaching to him about being safe in the streets was going unheard.

Often, while off to herself, she would think about how different things would be if she could bring her Mama back. A funny feeling came over her one day. She began reflecting back on Mama's (her mom) last words to her before she died. Mama had instructed her to take care of the family after she was gone. Carol-lou asked Mama a question. "Who's gonna take care of me Mama?" Mama replied, " Jesus will take care of you baby." In still believing those very words, with a heavy heart, Carol-lou instantly started to pray.

Nights when Verdell would come home late, as he lay sleeping Carol-lou would stand over him quietly listening and looking to make sure he was breathing. Not wanting to wake him she would pray: "Lord keep him safe in them streets, lead and guide him home to me safely." Oh how she loved that boy so dearly.

At age 19 Verdell became even more rebellious. He began telling Carol-lou, "Only Mama loved me." With tears in Carol-lou's eyes, all she could say was, "Son, I love you more." She would ask him, "Why do you think I preach and teach so much to you about the streets?" Yet still Verdell wouldn't listen. It seemed as though all Verdell cared about now was buying Jordan's, popping dollars and running the streets. More often now, with a disrespectful tone, he began telling Carol-lou how much she was tripping. With heaviness in her heart she never stopped praying and seeking God for his direction.

As Verdell would lay in his bed sleeping, Carol-lou would stand over him quietly listening and looking to make sure he was breathing. Not wanting to wake him she would pray: "Lord keep him safe in them streets, lead and guide him home to me safely." Oh how she loved that boy so dearly.

Verdell was 20 years old now. He was working and living in his own apartment. Though he had been through some hard times, such as joshes with jail and dealing with the loss of his grandmother, somehow it appeared that Verdell was pulling it all together. Realizing that he needed to really change his life, he decided to get baptized again and he also rededicated his life back to Christ.

IT WAS ME

    Where did the time go, Carol-lou wondered to herself. She was proud of the man he was becoming. She loved the way he cared and looked at his son, with so much love in his eyes. It brought back memories on how she would look at him when he was just a child. With joyful tears in her eyes, she turned away so he wouldn't see her and she prayed: "Lord keep him safe in them streets, lead and guide him home to me safely." Oh how she loved that boy so dearly.

    Verdell was 21 now, his second child was born

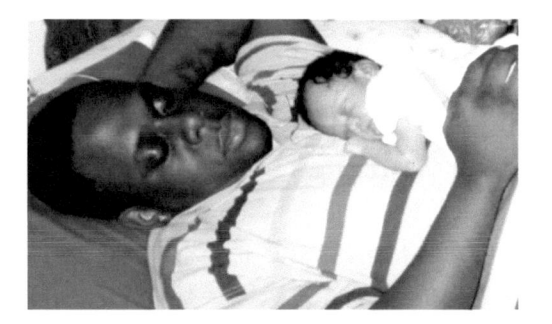

With that charming, beautiful smile he smiled at Carol-lou and said moms, "I's a man now"! Looking at him with love in her eyes, she replied, "Yes Verdell, God has blessed you". Setting new goals in his life Verdell moved back home with Carol-lou. Carol-lou was glad that Verdell was back home, but she still somehow had an uneasy feeling that something wasn't right. Supporting him in his decision, Carol-lou would help him in whatever way she could. It however was his birthday weekend and it was time to celebrate. Verdell and Carol-lou , along with some of his friends and family danced the night away. Carol-lou was trying to do some of Verdell's dances and he laughed. Oh how they celebrated! Looking at him from a distance she was amazed at how he had grown over the years, her Verdell was now 21. Looking much older than his friends, she laughed at how big he was for his age. She was proud that he was her son and eager to see what kind of father he would grow to be, for he had his whole life ahead of him. She prayed that God would lead his footsteps and make him into the man He wanted him to be. Months and days went by, and Verdell was doing fine. He was working hard, setting goals, and taking care of his family. Carol-lou was as proud as she could ever be. However, in knowing that he still needed prayers, before she would go to sleep at night she would pray: "Lord keep him safe in them streets, lead and guide him home to me safely". Oh how she loved that boy so dearly.

Mid-day Saturday morning, Verdell came over clowning and jokling with Carol-lou about going to an outside concert with her. Laughing and clowning with him she looked out the window and saw a familiar friend of Verdell's whom was someone she did not quite approve of . While looking out the window she said to him, "Verdell, I don't want you hanging with that boy, he gets in a lot of trouble. That boy will be the death of you". Verdell responded , "Mom he has no one else, his mom just died". With deep despair in her heart, she looked at him and sighed, understanding how he felt. He was taught as a child just as she was taught, to love everyone. Carol-lou kissed and hugged him tightly and said, "see you later", as she and her friend Valarie headed to the outside concert. It was such a beautiful Saturday evening. The sun shined brightly, so pretty that the day felt unreal. The concert was fun and long, but Carol-lou and Valerie were really having fun. Looking at the time she realized it had been a while since she had heard from Verdell. The last time she talked with him was to ask about his kids shoe sizes. She called and called his phone, but there was still no answer. Night fall came, and there was still no answer from Verdell. Carol-lou started feeling stabbing pains in her body, and she told Valerie that she was ready to go. She continued calling during her ride home, there was still no answer from Verdell. Once she made it home she took some medicine, and called Verdell one more time leaving him a message saying, "boy you better stop ignoring my calls", as he would often do, "you better come get them mattresses out my living room, call me". Trying not to worry, Carol-lou drifted off to sleep.

Loud knocks at the door awakened her from her sleep. She looked out the window and there stood two men dressed in black suits. As she answered the door, with tears in her eyes, seeing that it was the police she realized, "It was me". Verdell had been murdered. Feeling like she was in a dream, she began praying: "Lord keep him safe in them streets, lead and guide him home to me safely". Oh how she loved that boy so dearly.

While waiting on her sister Angel to come, and looking at the police with disbelief, she realized her Verdell was really gone. She began feeling that her prayers had gone unanswered, as she cried out loudly for Verdell. This time she cried knowing that he wasn't coming home to her safely, as she moaned.

As she sat on the pews at Verdell's funeral she thought to herself, "Lord I taught and preached to Verdell daily about them streets, was he listening"? She rose and walked to his casket, stood over him and whispered in his ear, knowing this time that she couldn't wake him. With tears in her eyes she said, "I did the best I could do Verdell", "Now Lord lead and guide him home to you safely, keep him wrapped in your arms safely". "Know that I loved that boy, and cared for him so dearly".

IT WAS ME

Carolyn Williams

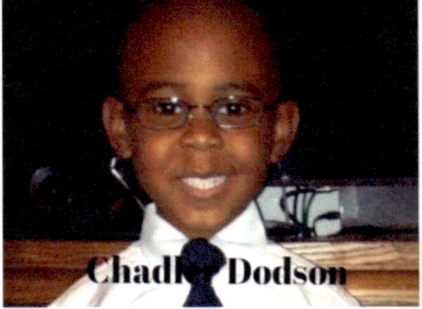

Unconditional Love

    We love and raise our children to the best of our ability. For being a parent doesn't come with instructions. Many times from infant to adulthood we fall and make numerous mistakes as we guide them through the process called "LIFE". This process is an unknown maze filled with uncertain obstacles. While sojourning through life; loving and teaching them, we pray that what we have taught them will stay, for the bible says, "Train up a child from whence they were trained and they shall never depart". Somehow I know that this is every parents prayer. However, we never expect that at any given day or time in a moment one can be reminded their children were only God's to loan.

Acceptance

I loan to you for yet a little while, a child of mine you called your own
For you will love them while they live, and mourn for them when they are gone
Months, days, hours, minutes and seconds, you will love them
Till I come for them; love on them, care for them, take care of them
Each were chosen and formed only for you, love them mercifully as I have loved you
They will give you a life time of uneventful memories filled with laughs and heartaches
Memories you will use to silence the pain
For this day I have chosen to usher them through the white pearly gates
Never did I promise when they were born that they would stay forever
Though your heart is filled with unimaginable emptiness and unbearable grief
I'll pray that you can say, eventually, after that unexpected day , "Thy will Lord, not mine"
Strengthen me to stand

Author: Lady C

The Formation of Healing Hearts

On November 2011, while in reading Deuteronomy 1:6, which stated, "The Lord our God spoke to us in Horeb, saying : "You have dwelt long enough at this mountain", Carolyn felt God was speaking directly to her. Carolyn felt as if God was telling her that for 4 years you have grieved behind your son, you have dwelt here long enough, and now is the time to start a grief support group. There are more families out there that are hurting and need your help. In not questioning God on the whys and how's, Carolyn says, "I picked up my tablet, wrote the vision, and made one phone call to a friend expressing my desires". That friend made one phone call and within the next hour Healing Hearts Grief Support Group was formed. I stayed on the phone till 2am that morning with a mother who had lost her son that January of 2011, to the senseless killing in the city of Baton Rouge, just as I had.

"Healing Hearts Grief Support Group is a grief support group based in Baton Rouge, La where grieving mothers and family members can come and share their feelings of grief in a safe, spiritual, private and confidential setting. Our motto is, "I'VE BEEN THERE". In order to know and identify with the pain of losing a mother, father, grandparents, and the ultimate gut wrenching loss; the loss of a child which was my son, you would have had to been there. "I've Been There". My prayer is to guide each family member to the Acceptance Stage of Grief. Healing Hearts is now a non-profit organization that supports the "Stop The Violence Movement". We participate in community and church events empowering families by educating them on the stages of grief and the effects grief and depression can have on your life.

For speaking engagements, counseling, monetary donations or more information about Healing Hearts please log onto Facebook under Healing Hearts Grief Support Group or through our web site hhgsg90.wix.com/2007. We welcome volunteers and sponsors that have the same love and drive as Healing Hearts does in supporting the cause of helping to end the senseless violence that is targeting our youth of today.

Testimonies

    Being a part of Healing Hearts has filled such a void in my life. It has afforded me the opportunity to meet people willing to listen and willing to help me without judging me or expecting me to get over my feelings, my pain and my memories. Healing Hearts has given me the avenue needed to meet with people who welcome my story. People that not only hear it, but they also share and embrace it. We all come together and help each other. Those individuals whom have been in pain for years are welcomed just as those whom have experienced it for the very first time. I was offered counseling and a group session when I first came to Healing Hearts and I received all of it and more with Healing Hearts in a way I never imagined.

Lena Benson

Testimonies

    My journey with Healing Hearts and Carolyn Williams started in March 2013. After meeting Carolyn, 3 years later my family and friend circle expanded. Carolyn has been there constantly encouraging me during those emotional times and spiritual battles. Battles that I know we all face from time to time. This woman has a heart of gold and will give her last. She is always giving ALL the Glory to God. She is always saying "Use Me Lord ", or "Lord ,it was you and I thank you "! Being in the presence of Carolyn just as a person, as well as being a part of Healing Hearts Grief Support Group has given me the understanding and knowledge on grief itself. It has also taught me how to help others. I would encourage anyone that's going through anything or that's grieving to come out and join in with Healing Hearts Grief Support Group!

Turoara (Tori) Matthews

Testimonies

    I would like to extend my heartfelt gratitude to the Director and Founder of Healing Hearts Grief Support Group, Carolyn Williams for helping me to grow. I thank Carolyn for pouring an increase of joy and laughter back into my life and into the lives of others around me. She is the mark of noble soul and refined character. The services she offered turned denial into acceptance, chaos into order, and confusion into clarity. Carolyn helped me to make sense of my past which bought a peace for today and created vision for tomorrow. My struggle has been hard, but through this process I have found great strength.

Rosalind Jenkins

Accepting God's Will

    To all the mothers, fathers and family members who have loss a love one to violence in the streets or through an uncontrollable circumstance. There are 5 stages of grief that we deal with daily: Anger, Denial, Bargaining, Depression and Acceptance. There is no specific time or day that you will experience them. Death is final, memories are forever. As you embark on this new unwanted journey that God has chosen you for, remember, it's not meant to be walked alone. Allowing yourself time to grieve is the most important vital stage of grief.
    The healing process begins when you become aware that you are experiencing the stages. Seek help, surround yourself with love, connect with someone who has been there, and make new memories by choosing to LIVE. Remain humble and allow God to use you. Listen for your assignment from the Lord, by forgiving and turning your tragedy into a victory. For the hole in your heart is there forever. It's up to you whether it will define you or break you. Allow God to work a healing in you. "It Was Me"

2 Chronicles 7:14 6:1(KJV)

If my people, which are called by My name would humble themselves, and pray and seek My face, and turn from their wicked ways, then I will hear from heaven, and will forgive their sin and heal their land.

Special Dedication to Mothers

On so many levels I am sure we can all relate. I have spoken with many mothers who too have lost their sons as I did to violence in the streets and each mother can honestly say that their children were getting ready to change their lives and give their lives back to Christ. As we embark on this journey that God has given us, I pray that God continues to humble you and use you. Do not let your child's death be in vain, for the hole in our spirits will be there for the rest of our lives. Your child can live on through your actions. Your child is gone, but there are other children out there such as your grandchildren, the neighborhood children, etc. who need you. I challenge you today to make a difference. Rise up and get involved in your community.

RISE UP AGAINST VIOLENCE, GRIEF & DEPRESSION

Resources:

Healing Hearts Grief Support Group- Counseling Service
Carolyn V. Williams- Mentor, Speaker, Author

DYPA Foundation- Specializing in Bullying-
Yalandra McClain-Mentor, Author, Speaker

Project Ride-Horse Therapy for at risk Youth
William "Bill" King- Mentor, Speaker

La Business Community Alliance-Educator on the How's and why's of Business
Harold Williams-Mentor, Speaker, Business Counselor

GoDjIdol-HipHop/R&B/Rap- DJ for all occasions, Mixologist, Studio Productions

IT WAS ME

Nicholas Menina
Photography, Video, Studio, Blog, Infomercial

Stop The Killing Inc.- Specializing in Educating the youth on Violence –
Arthur "Silky Slim" Reed-
Community Activist, Speaker, Mentor, Author

Carolyn V. Williams "Executive Director of Healing Hearts"

IT WAS ME

Made in the USA
Columbia, SC
16 March 2025